TO KEEP
THE HOUSE FROM
FALLING IN

ICHARD D'ABATE

TO KEEP
THE HOUSE FROM
FALLING IN

Richard D'Abate

an ithaca house book

Ithaca New York

Grateful acknowledgement is due the editors of
APPLE and EPOCH, in which some of these
poems first appeared.

Cover photograph by William Wilborn

ITHACA HOUSE
108 N. PLAIN ST.
ITHACA, N. Y.
14850

TABLE OF CONTENTS

I

II

III

I

AN EPITHALAMION
(for Bonnie)

Come to me memory and eyes,
bring people and the sun,
bring the night and houses,
bring animals, trees and books,
bring the wind and rain and sky:
help to adorn my most beautiful bride.

In my dream
you had married someone else.
He was a good Spic.
I couldn't ask you questions,
so I went to a blonde
who had your legs,
and a period.
But I went in
just the same.

    "Let no deluding dreams..."

It will be in St. Luke's,
at 11 o'clock in June.
There will be a mass.
Her grandmother gave us
a sewing machine
and embroidered linen.
My father is giving
the honeymoon,
in the Bahamas or St. Thomas.

"But let the night be calm..."
We will meet when the sky is dark,
when white flowers in the green are gone,
and will drink pink and yellow rain
on the cool side
of a marvellous Bermuda garden.

Fill me:
the space left
by the death of things
in my mind,
the space between then and now:
being a child and living now
in dreams of childhood,
dreams of manhood
and sex, dreams of you;
in distance, touch,
the sounds of things
and through my eyes
and in my eyes
the color of today.

I saw my mother this morning.
She told me how
before my grandfather died
he beat her mother,
breaking the bones in her hand.
And when the funeral ended
she came to our house.
And I heard her tell my mother
that, despite everything,
"You know you had a father."

The boys are smiling
to have found
a new pleasure,
and with wonder
at the first sight
of their liquid fragrant mella:
so white
against the pink and blue tiles
and the yellow toilet paper.

"...Perfection and a woman's name."

Then blood was down the young girl's leg.
At home she cried.
Her mother bathed and dried her,
and said that she was young
but now a part of things
and as good as any flower
growing in the ground.

I was playing with the little girl
who lived next door
to where I used to live,
and I hit her in the face,
by mistake,
and her father came outside
and yelled and said
"Do you this, look at her lips."
They were bleeding,
and I was afraid
because it was his daughter.

"Let no lamenting cries..."

Give me
for everything
that was never there,
for things that were there
but are now gone,
for the things
that are going.
Give me
between minutes,
between words and speech
and one day to the next.
Word to the minute,
to days and talking,
to memory and uncompleted time
give the life.
What I am.
What I am not.

I called for you.
A picture
of confusion
and a face,
breathing and
turning,
filled my hands.

I called for you.
The one who moved
away from me,
whose face was good,
was you.

I called to you.
I called for you.
A face had come.
A woman's face
I took for you.

Lose you by talking.
Lose you by talking.
I do not want to lose you,
by talking,
to the latin lover.

  "Let no deluding dreams...."

Can I touch your breast?
You answered yes.

And will you hold me there?
I'll hold you anywhere.

I said I thought it would be right.
Yes, please, come in tonight.

  "The bridal bowre and genial bed remain
  Without blemish or stain."

To have trouble in your womb
is not so bad.
And though your mother and hers
had trouble in the womb,
it is only natural
and no disgrace
to the child, man or woman
that brings it on.

"No let false whispers...."

Tears all fall,
a rubber ball,
two, four, five,
forgotten.

Sleepy eyes,
the cream of pies,
red, yellow, blue,
so thirsty:

Blown all away
for another day.
Wind, moon, sun, rain,
the doll's dress, the electric train.

Make me
into a thing
that will work,
despite whatever was
or might not.
Make me to think
that my space
is my own space
and not emptiness
but room to move around,
and if neither up or down
make it good
just to move around.
Make me move.

Make me meanings
for optical illusions,
for children,
for echoes,
for friends and a house,
for the houses of friends,
for unspent days and words
and time that moves
like a broken sentence.

A man who was bent and old,
began to cross the street with small steps.
He moved slowly and did not know
that the light had changed.
Cars pushed behind me not to wait.
So I drove around the man
who was old and intent on crossing.
And yet I know I should have waited,
at least until he reached the other side.

In the dream
my father would die
if the airport got his pills,
and though we had our troubles
I saved my father.
And because of that
it seems I was in bed
and you were underneath me,
speaking of a Spanish lover

who never said a word to anyone
but always made the kill.
And that was odd
because it seemed
that you were very happy
to have me in you.

I've been taken
for a Puerto Rican,
and was after all
as dark as they were.
I knew the tongue.
After many trips
on the uptown local
and so many looks,
I began to think
 that I could have
my pick
of the 96st. senoritas.

         "Ye damsels may be gone."

Will you take him?
He is so uneven.
Who for his lack
will say to you:
Clean my clothes.
Bring me food.
Lay down
and have a man,

the pain is yours.
Kiss me here.
I win my bread.

He is handsome,
and he will come,
and take me to his home.

On the soft bed
I'll hold his head,
and make him unafraid.

In the morning
he'll be a king
and speak to me of everything.

Lips nose breast teeth elbow bra,
or toothpaste feet hair panties toe,
finger eyes the rump and penis,
and underpants and nipple nails and tongue,
vagina knee ear period pad,
the vaseline navel toilet shampoo,
hairpin tub and mirror stubble cream,
the ankle neck razor pubic hair lash.

In her dream
I asked
how did you expect to build a home
on the shape of a curve?
There, only one point is
for balance;

at any other place
we will slide down
off the edge of the earth
and our house will crumble
in the darkness
and our children will have
crippled minds,
and then they will die
and we will die.
But she must have been thinking
of a house we once saw
in the shape of a curve.
So on must mean in,
and, after all,
we may find
some flat place.

    "...thou night so long expected."

If I am throwing
sand on your leg
and you say to stop
but I keep on,
will you turn on me
when we are together?

And if I stop,
will I clean you off,
or go toward the water,
annoyed at your stand

and wash my hands
when we are together?

If we lie in the sun
will you fall asleep in the afternoon,
and will I cover you?
Or if I fall asleep in the afternoon,
will you cover me
when we are together in the afternoon?

     "and this is my friend."

Take me
out of myself
and into yourself
and into myself.
Take me away.
Take me home.
Take meat to me,
milk and fruit,
salt sugar bread.
Take chance,
knowing
I will not fail you,
knowing
I will fail you.
Take care of me
that I can expect
everything I ask of you,
that I can expect
nothing I ask of you.

Take time
so that we can talk
about these things.

"This day is holy; do ye write it down."
And I am writing, though I might lose you
to the latin lover through too much talk.
And yet it is quite clear that at times
I have been seen in the Spanish bull ring
of an Italian movie, with curling black hair,
with open white shirts, with bronze skin,
with graceful hips, doing the act of the ring.
And so I may prove mysterious by this poem.

Pajama top to eye hello and so then
to frying pan glass dish sink and cook
for your old friend good juice flakes
or scrambled things in whipping bowls
and jello fork to cake a salad boon
for friends of basting broiling tops
or glazed in time a chill serves 2
I like them raw or hard hello kiss kiss.

I am your man.
The white flower man.
The cigar man.
I will rescue you
from the burning porch.

I will strangle the thin gray man.
He cannot touch you.
I will give you the jewels and makeup.
All the white dresses
and pierced ears.

We will leave by the drain pipe.
We will laugh at the room boxes.
The car will never hit the wall.
I will never take her out.
We will always ride the white subway.

PIE

What a pie our first pie.
It was made with peaches,
three pounds of peaches.
And the crust was brown,
the crust was thin and flaky.
My wife and I
made that pie.

HAWK'S SHADOW

The hawk's shadow
has frightened the city mouse,
and he hides away
under the third rail.

The city mouse
eats droppings
of gray pigeons
flying over the library.

Starlings will kill
the city mouse
as he runs along
the cement curb.

HAWKS ARE IN THE AIR

Hawks are in the air
and I think
for all you care
that they want to kill a mouse.

Hawks are in the air
but just think
of mouse despair
and the grip of tightening claws.

Hawks are in the air
and it's more
than we should bear
to let the hawks
to let the hawks
fall upon us from the air.

THE SKATING RINK

We moved on the ice
in long ovals.
I watched the good ones
to see how it was done,
but almost tripped on a girl
who had fallen down.
I helped her up.
A man and woman were together:
he held her waist
as they both went slowly around.
One girl spun herself,
making deep cuts
in the middle ring.
I slowed to rest.
And there was a man
like water on the ice
whose hat was everywhere.

CORELLI CAME

I sat.
His music
was my dream.
And music was
this dream
to me.

Arcangelo,
the Italian man,
my violin,
Corelli came;
in heart's arm
held me
with hand's mouth
sung:

Ricardo you
my man shall be,
shall passion time
as beautifully,
and in the palace
of ancestral wolf
with honored rhyme
will work your truth.

I sat
and knew
what I had done,
and what proud thing
this dream music was,
but there was need
that I should sing
and name my name
and call myself
a son.

II

JOHN BERGER POEMS

our father on the sea
hose trips brought black
frica back, tattoos
d boat promises
r months
 remember
imals carved
ys to entice
lms of giraffe
d South American spears
d love,
erchant Marine love
r your mother
ho was pretty
 thought,
d loneliness
 seemed
 apartment dark
r your mother
d you
d, for me
ho watched
er easy face
d child's eyes
reak and choke
n a stuttering tongue

while your head turned away,
mystery
and a young pain
to think of the why
of this waiting.

II

You were never on the sea
though you wanted boats
and had one once.
You were in the subway
with me.
We were lost,
your face was crying
against my bravado.
I called my father
for instructions,
your face was smiling.
We found a train for home.
The doors began
to close on me
as you went in.
I looked
and saw
the eye of fear
was moving
in your face:
eye that saw the subway

ride for years
in underwater tubes
saw blind saxophonists play
and violins fall and dogs
men and shoes
into the ice wheel flames
heat lit stations
that had no names
saw dark intestine stops
the mascara crowds
penises red lips and nails
saw drawn vaginas
and poster boards
of the boat show's white sails
and saw
despite so many men
that you would be left
in the subway
alone again.

III

There was nothing in my house
to compare
with what was in his house;
my house
barren always
of exotic promise.

I waited to go to his house
to be in that place of things,
an only child's
heaping paradise,
to play with his
mahogony hydroplane
to move the twin levered
transformer of trains
to touch and hold
the animal hide shield
and warrior's spear.

And to see
in the other room
on chests and dresser tops
egrets and elephants,
fine antelope
and smooth gazelles
and rhinos carved
to a perfect finish
waiting in the dark
heat of the living room
African hunters,
baobab stained black,
with cut faces
clean muscles
and spears thin shafted

in boney hands
held, holding
wooden menace.

While we were on the fire escape
shooting at pigeons with a BB gun
when his mother wasn't home,
and making his hamster eat seeds
to watch its cheeks fill up.
He had to offer me the hamster
because his mother didn't like to hear it
run at night, though hamsters
are supposed to run at night.

I brought it home.
But it didn't hold my interest
very long.
My mother or my sister
put him in the cellar.
I didn't change his cage
or give him water,
I didn't give him food.
I let him die
under the draft
and half light
of our cellar window.

25

"You are wrong
in what you've done"
my mother said
to me.

IV

Once I held him
in my room
with my knee
in his chest,
my bayonet
at his neck,
and with mock fire
made to kill him
on the bed.

His body was soft
soft and heavy
with surprise
and his eyes,
jewels of fear,
rolled.

But he yelled
and burned you see
as if he thought
my play was real.

I let him up
and laughed at him
across the room
to think that I would hurt him
in some way.

And now
that I look at you
again,
and see your face
as I lifted myself away,
I cannot
meet your eye
as then.
I turn
to other friends
who know me as I am
and say:
he did not see
the joke in me.

V

Your father brought it home,
I thought.
Six months
of tattooed semen
panther eagle
dragon boa

screaming for the flow
eat and hunt
breath twisting
up the river
great zoo
or place
of release.

He fell overboard at a boat party
a few nights after he came back.
He hurt his side and his head.
Too drunk to stand
was the jungle king.
He seemed like such a fool to me.

See where she waits
now ship in port
her love is safe
from evil lands.

See where he comes
with guiding star
and bring some things
to melt her heart.

See where they sit
their home and nest
perhaps content
that love is rest.

VI

I was on the subway
going home for a weekend.
Most of the train was empty.
The doors opened and closed.
The train stood for a minute,
someone walking on the platform stopped.
He looked at me and I looked at him.
His fat body was gone from him;
he was tall and looked handsome.
The train began to move.
I waved and he waved;
his face was smiling.
I had not seen him
in a long time.
He went upstairs.
I didn't see him again.
The train moved into the tunnel
and went under the river.
It came up on the other side
     I was happy to see him
and traveled above ground.
It went under again
just before the last stop.
     I have not seet him again
I went up the stairs into the street
     I was happy to see you
and took a bus home.

VII

Once
after these poems were done
I thought I saw you
walking on the street.
I became afraid
that we would meet
and afraid that what I 'd said
would all become untrue.
But he turned,
John Berger,
and it was not you.

COMET

Comet through the east sky
I saw in the morning
with other stars moving ways
that were not apparent to me.
If in the stars there was inspiration
or other old enthusiasms,
I could not feel the presence.
Only a comet in the sky I knew.

The dog had to pee the moonlight,
it was by an accident then
that we looked into the sky,
morning moon sky at that time
of night a thing we did not recognize
it's place, or name any explanation.
The dog smelled like wet grass
and did not notice the heavens.

Perhaps better to forget the sky.
Another obsecure poet said so too.
My wife's body is warm and the sheets:
these are things you know,
but if I speak only to myself,
about the sky and in truth or
inspiration what we ever know there
I now say the comet has my eye.

I say it appears and disappears
and that it holds its own in darkness,
breaks order and rotation
the dumbness of the stars.
It shows itself to animals that don't see,
and that it may never return,
and that it blinds me like a fool
in the hope of accidental ecstacy.

III

OSPREY

I dreamt of the osprey,
not as he is bonebreaker,
but in his gliding moment
above the lake edge holding
my eye and the air in my dream.

To everyone I said: look
look, there is the osprey,
see him as I have pointed.
It was good to be the one,
even for the people in a dream.

But I could tell them no more,
no explanation in the offering,
what thing to gain from knowing,
or why the speaking brought elation,
only that it was, and there it was.

They turned on my finger
and looked into the sky.
All who were there said: yes
osprey, the body and the wing.
And I was not despised in my own dream.

WHEN I COME OUT OF THE HOUSE

When I come out of the house
the carpenter bee drops two levels
of hovering.

When I come out of the house
chipping sparrows leave the porch
of sunlight.

When I come out of the house
my dog lifts up her head
from the green grass.

When I come out of the house
the wind blows the shadow of my clothes
on the ground.

WILLIAMS

I was reading Williams
in the laundromat.

Later on it rained,
wetting my red car,

water also finding the leaves
but no tulips in them,

and, waiting for her wash
with a hat on,

one woman was left
at the station.

THREE PROPOSITIONS

PROPOSITION 1

If an old cripple says to you
that in '26 or '36 there was a flood
and he jumped in the car, went down
got her, got rope, kept the house
from falling in where the bridge
washed down the creek you are
standing in front of right now
and that further up his orchard was
and down there he kept the cows,
the garden being where your house is
and how he always used to mow
the patch in back belonging to the
German lady but when she moved off
he stopped and then his legs went bad
but he every year picks the black caps
still when they commence to be ripe
and that, O, there are a lot of things
a lot of things he could tell you,
then you should listen,
and you should believe
that old man because
that is all he has to tell you,
and it is the truth.

PROPOSITION 2

If an old cripple comes to you
with cucumbers in his hat to give you
saying that it doesn't rain much now
because when they shoot people to space
or shoot up the moon something happens
everytime in the world something bad
an earthquake or such changes the weather
and that once you could have seen plain as day
Europe Asia and Africa on the moon but not now
and the clouds aren't as high as they used to be
so the sky is confused by what men are doing
and it don't rain much at all now,
then, first, take the cucumbers,
and talk with him
and consider the reason
of what he has said.
Consider with this old man
the dark connections
of weather and circumstance.
Say to him finally
that he is right.
Say this because
your explanation is
no better than his,
because you are strange
in your own way,
because cucumbers will grow,
and because the rain
that falls upon his head
falls also upon yours.

PROPOSITION 3

If an old cripple comes and asks you
because his son don't come around too often
and having no car himself he can't
get around with his legs the way they are
could you please he would be much obliged
if you were to take him to town with you
to get the length of spring he needs
for what he rigged up on the mower
and that his wife you know keeps her eye
on the sales when they're having them
which can save a man a lot of money
so that when you are going in you might
take her with you to the supermarket
she won't be long in there,
then say what you please
to that old man,
but do not help him.
He is an old man, and a cripple.
He will drag you down.
He will make you serve.
He will be a leech
and take your life away.
He knows no life but his own.
Turn your back on him.
The needs of the old
are extavagant,
and have no boundary.
Let his son take him to town.

IN THE LINE

In New York my grandmother is dying,
and that will leave my mother with no mother
so that her flesh will be alone in the city.
My sister is there and I am here,
but we are out of her as she is out of her mother,
and are not for her in the same way as her
mother is,
and are not in the same way as our mother,
except that we will become that way:
singular flesh, orphans in the sixtieth year
who shiver in the draft of the hole
that suddenly fell open behind them.

Then embracing the absence of history,
she will sleep closer to my father
who is not her flesh, but her promise in the dark.
To whose comfort I cannot come,
flesh is no promise to flesh,
I cannot give what is not mine to give
the comfort of time being only forward,
and I am broken with them already.
I am set away from the edge
to build my strength against that time,
to make my promise against that time
when I will become as the very beginning of
things,
and the very guardian of the empty hole.

$2.95

Richard D'Abate was born in New York City in 1946. He was graduated in 1967 from Columbia College of Columbia University magna cum laude in English Literature and Phi Beta Kappa, received an M.F.A. from Cornell University in 1971, and is continuing work on a Ph.D. degree in medieval and Renaissance literature while teaching English at Nasson College in Springvale, Maine. He was married to Bonnie Randolph in 1968 and has one daughter, Leah.

Other recent books in the Ithaca House Poetry Series include:

Rochelle Nameroff   *Body Prints*
Eric Torgersen   *At War with Friends*
Alvin Greenberg   *Dark Lands*
Jerald Bullis   *Taking Up the Serpent*
                                        all $2.95

Look for these forthcoming books:

Steve Katz   *Cheyenne River Wild Track*   cloth $4.95 paper $2.95   August 30, 1973
Ray DiPalma   *Soli*   cloth $4.95   paper $2.95 Sept. 15, 1973
Warren Woessner   *Landing*   cloth $4.95   paper $2.95   Oct. 1, 1973
Lynn Shoemaker   *Coming Home*   cloth $4.95 paper $2.95   Oct. 1, 1973
David Gitin   *City Air*   cloth $4.95   paper $2.95 Nov. 1, 1973
Roger Skillings   *Alternative Lives*   (short stories) cloth $5.95   paper $3.95   Nov. 1, 1973